Illustrated by

Bob Bampton
Jim Channell
Paula Chasty
Sue Gibson
Ian Jackson
Steve Kaye

Cover illustration

Richard Orr

Acknowledgements

ARDEA, title page (P Steyn), **BRUCE COLEMAN**: 25U (H Albrecht). **FRANK LANE**: 16U (M. Newman); 17U (W Wisniewski); 17C (A Christiensen); 20U (L W Walker); 23U (R P Lawrence). **NHPA**: 11U (M Leach); 14U (Agence Native); 15UR (J Jeffery); 15UL (P Johnson); 21B (S Dalton); 22U (J & M Bain); 27U (H Teyn); 32B (A Bannister); 32U (B Wood). **SEAPHOT**: 29B (H Voigtmann); 31B (H Voigtmann). **SURVIVAL ANGLIA**: 28U (J & D Bartlett); 28B (J & D Bartlett); 30U (J Foott); 35B (T & L Bomford).

ISBN 1 85854 143 3

Published by Brimax Books Ltd, Newmarket, England 1994
Printed in Spain

Somewhere to Sleep

Written by
Karen O'Callaghan & Kate Londesborough

BRIMAX · NEWMARKET · ENGLAND

Contents

Animal builders

Animals make their homes in every kind of place, hot or cold, wet or dry.

tailor bird

wasp

harvest mouse

badger

beaver

Animals use different parts of their bodies as tools. Their sharp beaks, strong legs, teeth and claws can build, weave and dig.
Their homes are made of all kinds of materials. They may use grass, leaves, twigs, mud, wood, shells or stones.

Making homes

In and under a tree

Many animals make their homes in trees. The homes are not always the same. Animals may use the leaves, the branches, the trunk or even the roots of a tree.

sugar glider

penduline tit

orang-utan

heron

red squirrel

raccoon

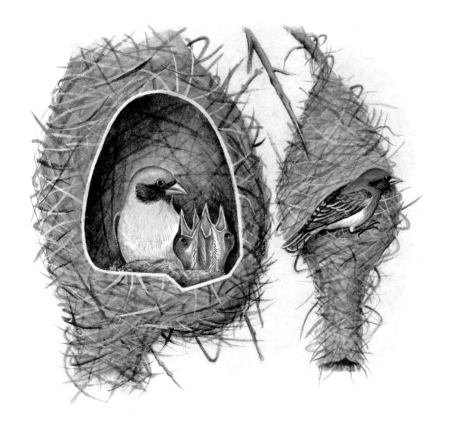

Red-headed weaver birds have two homes. The male builds a strong nest for the female to lay her eggs in. He makes another nest for himself close by. The family use these nests for many years.

A **badger's** underground home is called a set. The entrance is often under the roots of a large tree. Using their sharp claws and powerful front legs, badgers dig tunnels sloping downwards. The tunnels end in large chambers. Some are used for storing food, others for living and sleeping in.

Under the ground

Some other animals make their homes underground. Here they are protected from bad weather. They are also safely hidden from enemies. Many of these animals are powerful diggers.

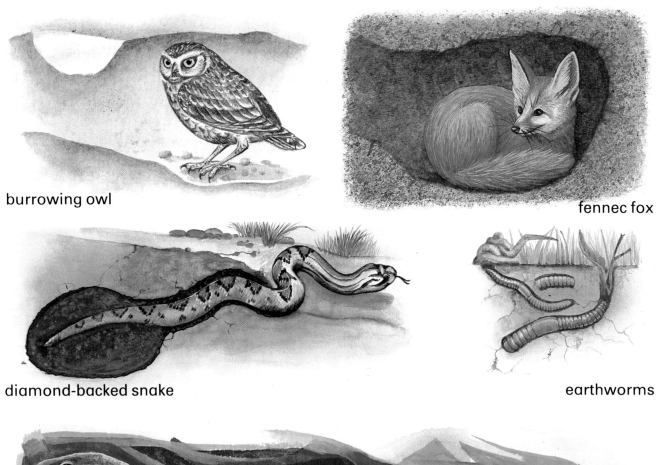

burrowing owl

fennec fox

diamond-backed snake

earthworms

komodo dragon

Rabbits dig burrows, tunnels and escape holes. Their home is called a warren. Female rabbits line special nursery burrows with their own fur.

A **mole's** home is a hollowed-out nest underground. It is lined with leaves and grass. From the nest, the mole digs many tunnels. Using its sharp claws and strong front legs, it loosens the earth. The mole then turns itself in the tunnel and pushes the loose earth up and out to the surface. This makes a small hill above the ground.

The **chuckwalla** lives in the desert. At night, it digs a hole in the sand to sleep in, protected from cold desert nights.

Many **snakes** living in the desert escape the heat of the day by pushing themselves into the sand.

Jerboas also make a burrow deep under the desert sand where it is cool. The jerboa digs two tunnels leading to the surface. As it enters one tunnel, the end is blocked up with sand. If a **snake** follows it, the jerboa can escape, using the second tunnel.

Near water

Animals that live near rivers dig out their homes in the riverbank.

An **otter's** home is called a holt. Otters dig out a holt in the bank of a river or under the roots of a tree. The entrance tunnel is under the water. It slopes upwards, ending in a large, dry chamber lined with moss and grass.

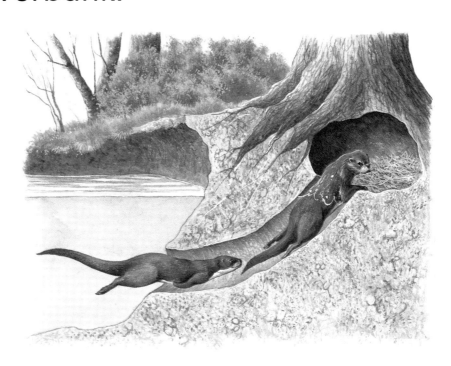

The **kingfisher** uses its sharp, pointed beak to make a tunnel in the riverbank. It lines the nesting chamber with fish bones.

A **pond tortoise** digs into the soft mud at the edge of a pond to make a home for the winter.

Under water

Some animals build homes in water. They are special builders.

The **water spider** spins a bell-shaped web around water plants. It collects air bubbles on its hairy body and carries them underwater. It squeezes the air into the web with its back legs, making many journeys to do this. It eats and sleeps in this underwater home.

Beavers use their sharp teeth to chop down trees. They stick branches and stones together with mud to make a dam across a river. Behind the dam the beavers build a lodge. The nest is above water. Food is stored underwater. The entrances are underwater so the beavers can reach their food even when the water is frozen over.

In high places

Nests in cliffs or on rocky ledges make very safe homes.

These **bee-eaters** make their homes in sandy cliffs. They dig out a nesting hole with their strong beaks. Many bee-eaters live close together.

Golden eagles build nests for their young on rocky ledges high up in the mountains. They weave a nest of twigs which they return to every year.

Puffins spend most of their time in the sea, but they make a home for their young in the cliffs. Using their beaks and feet they make a long tunnel. At the end of this tunnel they dig out a large nesting chamber.

A home together

Some animals live together in large groups. It is safer and they can help each other to make homes.

Prairie dogs live together in towns underground. They build a raised mound at each entrance hole so that rain water cannot flood their tunnels. They clear away all the grass and plants growing near their homes so that enemies cannot creep up on them. Guards watch out for any danger.

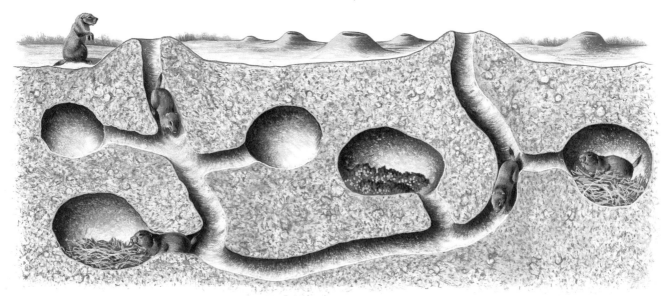

Deep underground, each animal has its own nesting chamber. These are joined by tunnels leading to storerooms where food is kept for the winter.

Social weaver birds join together to build a huge home. They weave grasses to make a roof. Under this roof each pair of birds builds a bottle-shaped nest. Every year, new nests are built under the old ones.

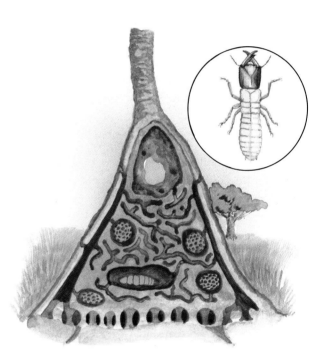

Millions of **termites** live together in huge towers which they build out of earth and mud. The mud is baked by the hot sun and becomes rock hard.

Inside the mound there are living rooms, storerooms and nurseries for the young. All the termites have the same mother and father, who live together in the largest chamber in the middle of the nest. Blind workers build the nest and collect food. Soldier termites guard the nest.

Sharing a home

Sometimes different animals live together, sharing the same home.

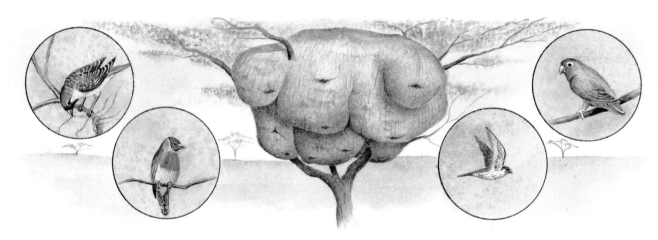

At times, the **social weaver birds** are joined by other birds. **Red-headed finches, pygmy falcons** and **lovebirds** make their homes in empty nests.

The **osprey** or **fish hawk** builds a large nest with sticks and branches at the top of a dead tree. Smaller birds like **wrens** or **sparrows** build their homes in the side of this nest. Although the osprey is a bird of prey it eats only fish, so all the birds live happily together.

This bird called a **sooty shearwater** shares its burrow with a **tuatara**. The tuatara is very slow moving and too lazy to make its own home. It does not harm the bird. They can share a home because the bird searches for food in the daytime and the tuatara hunts at night.

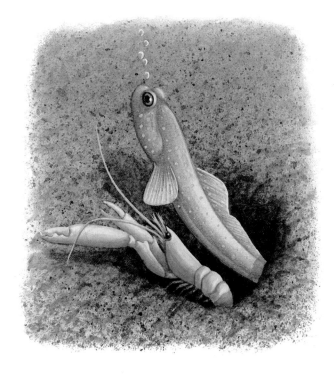

This **pistal prawn** digs a burrow in the sand and shares it with a **goby fish**. The goby sits in the entrance to the hole keeping watch. If an enemy approaches, the fish disappears inside the burrow warning the prawn to hide as well.

Any hole is home

Some animals do not build their own homes. They use any hole or burrow they can find.

The hole in this cactus was made by a **woodpecker**. When the woodpecker left its nest the **elf owls** moved in.

The **burrowing owl** makes its nest in the burrow of another animal. Sometimes it will share with the animal. This owl lives with **prairie dogs**. It spends most of its time outside the burrow looking for food.

This **blenny fish** lives anywhere it can find shelter – a crack in the rock, under stones, even in a broken bottle.

The **striped hyena** lives in caves or old buildings. Animal bones at the entrance show where the hyena's den is.

The **spotted hyena** makes its home in an empty anteater's nest.

This **red fox** has found an empty hole. Inside it has made tunnels and chambers. Its home is called an earth. The fox spends most of the daytime inside, going out at night to hunt.

Carrying a home

These animals do not need to build a home. They carry it with them.

The **garden snail** has a shell which is part of its body. Wherever the snail goes, its shell gives it shelter and protection.

The **tortoise** also has a shell. It grows bigger as the tortoise grows. When in danger, the tortoise pulls its head and legs up into the shell. The hard shell protects its soft body.

This female **wallaby** does not carry her own home but carries a special home for her baby. The baby lives in a pouch on the mother's stomach for many months.

This **turtle** lives in rivers. The turtle can rest on the river bottom and stretch its long neck up out of the water to breathe. If an enemy comes near, it pulls back into its shell.

Moving house

As some animals move from place to place they must build or find new homes to live in.

Killer bees fly in swarms searching for food. Wherever they land, the bees find a new home. This may be an empty box, a tin can, a crack in a building, or an empty burrow.

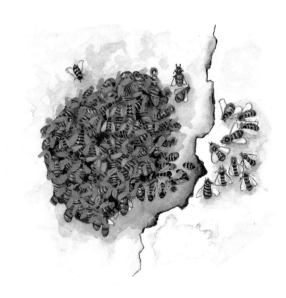

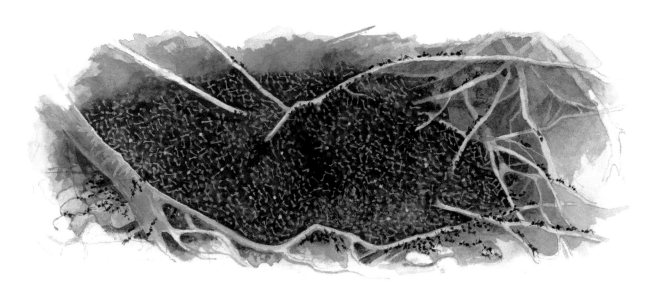

These **army ants** also carry out swarm raids, sometimes staying up to three weeks in one place. Here they make homes in hollow trees or under rocks. Thousands of ants hook onto each other to make a kind of tent. The queen ant and her eggs are safe inside.

Chimpanzees move around in the forest searching for food. Every night they sleep in a new place. They build a nest high in the trees. Each animal builds a platform made of broken branches and then bends twigs over it for a roof. The chimpanzee uses leafy branches to make a soft bed on this platform.

The **hermit crab** does not grow its own shell. It lives in empty whelk shells. When the crab grows too big for one shell it searches for a bigger one. It measures the new shell with its front claws. If it is the right size, the crab climbs in.

A home for the babies

Some animals that do not have a home for most of the year will build a home when they have babies.

Ovenbirds make strong mud nests that are windproof and waterproof. They build from the bottom of the nest upwards in layers ending in a dome shape.

The female **king cobra** makes a nest hidden in the forest. She collects leaves to make a soft bed. She coils herself around her eggs to keep them warm.

Hornbills make a safe home for their young in a hole in a tree. The mother bird stays inside the nest with her chicks. Here they are safe from attack by snakes and monkeys. When the chicks are ready to fly she breaks open the nest to free them all.

Brown bears make a winter den. The bear either digs a den under a rotten tree or finds a cave. It spends the winter asleep and has its cubs in the spring.

The **dormouse** always has a home but makes an extra one for its babies.

During the winter the dormouse has an underground home. It sleeps rolled in a ball wrapped in grass. In spring the dormouse makes a new home. It builds a loosely woven nest of grass. When the dormouse has babies, it makes a special nursery nest. This nest is bigger and is lined with soft moss and leaves.

Home is a safe place

Animals must always be on the look out for danger. They may be the next meal for a hungry hunter. These animals build special homes to protect themselves or their babies.

The **mourning dove** makes its nest deep in the spines of a cactus. The sharp spines protect the eggs and the baby birds from enemies.

This **gambels quail** builds its nest under clumps of prickly pear cactus. The sharp spines help to keep lizards away. The male guards the tunnel to this spiky home.

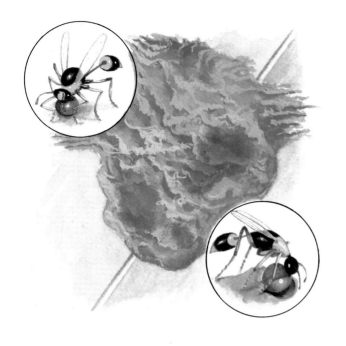

This **mud-dauber wasp** collects soft, wet mud with its front legs and builds a nest for its egg. The wasp seals up the entrance hole by spreading runny mud over it with its jaws. The mud dries hard in the hot sun and the egg is safe inside.

The **caddis fly larva** builds a tube around its soft body made of small stones or shells. Inside this armour it is safe from water spiders. Fish may not see it hidden against stones of the riverbed. As it grows, the larva adds more pieces to its tube.

The **garden eel** digs a tube-like hole in the sea bed. It floats upright held firm in the sand by its tail. If in danger, it disappears quickly into its hole. It never leaves the safety of its home.

Somewhere to sleep

Some animals have a special resting place for sleeping.

Sea otters have no special home. They live in groups close to the shore near beds of seaweed called kelp. When they want to sleep, they wrap themselves up in the long strands of seaweed. This stops them from drifting away from each other.

The **rainbow parrot fish** spins a web around itself when it settles down to sleep.

Snow leopards live high in the mountains. They hunt at night. During the day, the leopard finds a place to rest. This is called its lair. It may be in a cave or under a hollow tree.

Reef sharks are fierce hunters. Sometimes they swim into caves for a rest. In the caves they lie very still but they are not asleep. Their eyes are always open. These sharks become calm and peaceful when they are resting.

Hidden attackers

The **moray eel** ambushes animals from its home. The eel lives in a crack in the rock. When a fish or a lobster swims past, the eel darts out and catches it.

The **octopus** lives on the sea bed which is covered in rocks and stones. Often an octopus will move stones around itself to make a lair. It hides in the lair, darting out to catch food.

The **trapdoor spider** digs a burrow covered by a lid. In the daytime, the spider hides in its burrow. At night it opens the lid a little and watches. When the spider sees its prey, it springs open the lid and dashes out.

Scorpions live in rocky cracks or burrows in the sand. They dig deep into the sand with their front legs to hide from the hot desert sun. At night, they come out to hunt.

Unusual homes

These are some of the strange homes animals have.

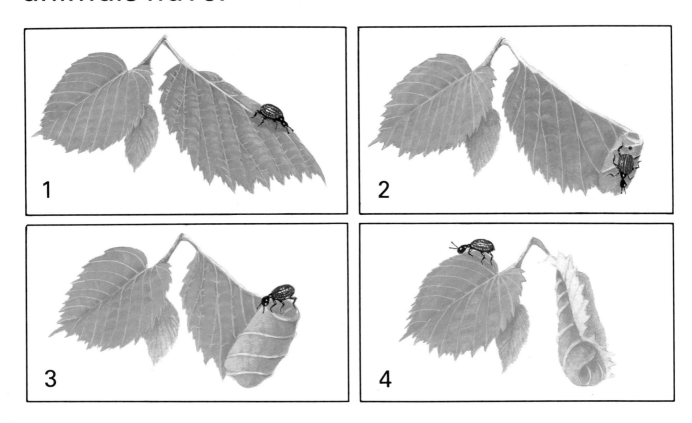

1
2
3
4

This **leaf-rolling weevil** makes a home for its egg. It uses a leaf that is still growing on the branch of a tree. It rolls and twists the leaf, wrapping its egg safely inside.

This little **pearl fish** has a home inside the body of another animal. The **sea cucumber** is a long tube-like animal. At night, the pearl fish swims about searching for food. It then wriggles back inside the sea cucumber and hides.

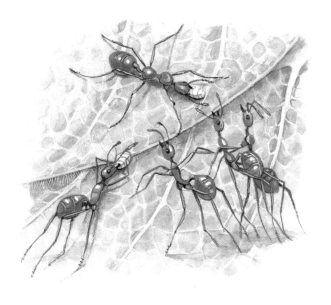

Weaver ants use their young grubs to help them make a nest. The grubs make silk in their mouths. As some of the ants pull leaves together, others holding the grubs, criss-cross from side to side. The silk sticks the leaves together making a waterproof home.

These **ants** bite tiny holes in the thick thorns of a tree and make their nest inside.

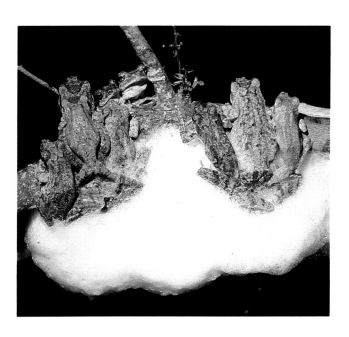

These **frogs** make their nest by beating egg jelly from inside their bodies into a foam using their back legs. The nest is on a branch over the water. The outside of this foam nest hardens to protect the eggs inside. Later, the nest softens. Tadpoles wriggle out and drop into the water below.

Nature's builders

These animals are expert builders. Each one uses its body in a different way.

The **leaf-curling spider** makes a leaf shelter next to its web. Using a silk thread the spider spins silk across the leaf. As the silk dries it shrinks. This curls the leaf into a tube shape. This spider could be called one of the engineers of the animal world.

The **sandmason worm** makes an underwater burrow in the sand. Above its hole it builds a 'tree' of sand to trap its food. It picks up sand grains one at a time with its tentacles and sticks them together making the tree shape.

Many other animals are clever builders.

The **tailor bird** makes its nest by sewing together two leaves. The bird makes holes along the edges of the leaves with its sharp beak. It threads grass through the holes to join the nest together. Inside, a soft bed is made with grass.

The **harvest mouse** builds a home from wheat grass. It balances on a stalk, holding on with its back legs and tail. It then weaves strips of wheat grass round the plant stalk to make a nest.

Homes of all shapes and sizes give animals warmth, shelter and protection. They are places in which to eat, sleep and raise a family.